M

Hafsah Khan-Cheema

BookLeaf Publishing

Moments © 2023 Hafsah Khan-Cheema

All rights reserved.

No part of this publication may be reproduced, stored in a retrieval system, or transmitted, in any form or by any means, electronic, mechanical, photocopying, recording or otherwise, without the prior written permission of the presenters.

Hafsah Khan-Cheema asserts the moral right to be identified as author of this work.

Presentation by *BookLeaf Publishing*

Web: www.bookleafpub.com

E-mail: info@bookleafpub.com

ISBN: 9789358316209

First edition 2023

To my parents

Who fill me with unconditional love every day

PREFACE

In my profession as a doctor, one thing I lack is artistic expression when working. Writing poetry has taught me so much about the freedom of creativity and how to craft beautiful words from emotions. By doing so, I have been able to create a snapshot of my life and how I view the world. I have only just begun my journey into the magical world of poetry and I am excited to see what the future holds.

Running

Shoes on
Warm rays extending, battling to erase the storm
of yesterday
Brightening the world around it
A twinge in my knee whilst I focus on the
rhythm
of my breathing
The forest beckons
Freedom. At last!
Cooler, crisper air floods my lungs
Sunlight competes with golden leaves
It is losing

A family meal

Steaming pots laden with pulao and salans
Chicken, kofte
Curated by the head of the table,
my mother
(my vibrant salad a tribute to her genius)
Laughter, conversations flowing:
witty remarks, rehashing memories and recent
trips abroad
Loud proclamations of career ambitions
or abandonment
Past, present, future
The zesty ordered mayhem
Time for dessert!

Morning

Bright harsh sunlight invades through the blinds
Its angry footsoldiers battling off any remaining
shadow
They poke me with their swords
Stirring me from my slumber
I writhe against the army
And drift

Coffee with a friend

The floral, nutty scent caresses the air
Gently kneading in waves of calm
The hours pass as quickly as
a bee gathering nectar
To produce the sweetest of honey-
dripping laughter
Sparkling eyes of joy
like light bouncing off the endless sea
Filled to the brim with love and grief and pain
and understanding
Like gannets, we dip in and out of each others
lives
Connected till the end

Baking

People ask me why I love to bake
Is it for the flavours I create?
The balance of sweet, salt and sour?
Or the relaxing process of my labour?

For me, it is the triumph when what I make
Turns out a spitting image of what I undertake
The same ingredients for endless possibilities
I admit I am a critic of my own abilities

So sharing my dishes with those around me
Sweetens the praise and makes it more tasty

The funeral

It is the day of the funeral
The air has on a formal, fresh attire
And even the sky has darkened, tipped its hat
in respect

His widow furnished in black
Moves, breathes, as the world keeps reeling
Clear eyed she says
He has gone to Heaven now.
He is in a better place.

Sleeping

Sleeplessness
Insomnia
Keeps me awake
The world running through my head
Events from the day
My future plans
Fears and hopes
Swirling around, tormenting me
Hounding me
Their barks echoing at dawn
Drowsiness
Hypersomnia

Tree

Time passes differently for me
My long, ropy branches stretching out
as I yawn in the morning light
Birds flit about my leaves
Stopping for a quick chat with a friend
or nestling by my trunk
Watching as I slowly undress with the season
My roots snuggled deep into the soil below
a network, a catch up with my neighbours,
family and beyond.
Eager to hear of the latest news
or gossip
You may assume I am a passive, patient prop
There is nothing further from the truth

Death

A hushed whisper
furtive glances
downcast eyes
I am not to be mentioned
Locked in that box at the back of your head
Don't speak of me too loudly else the
shadows will spread
across the walls, engulfing everything
in its path

But when you open the box and speak of me
freely
You will see that I am not the enemy
My power is diluted, lost to the wind
I am a part of life

Foraging

It is something magical
when you see
from nothing but dirt, light and water
and from a seed
grows a shoot, rising up
in its desperation to be stronger, better
And when it has matured bearing gifts
bask in the vibrancy, taste the juice of success
To use, cook, transform
Connected, grounded, earthed
A full cycle

Microaggression

A lingering look
Sets me apart from others
You do not belong

Islam

Tranquility
Dangling rope in the murky dark
Accepting my fate

Goals

When I was young
I aspired to be the
best possible version of myself

Now I realise I am surrounded by people
who are in need of a helping hand
along the way

When I am old
I want others to be
standing on my shoulders
amongst the stars

Free Palestine

Bombs rain down
drenching the innocent
fleeing for safety

Children covered in soot
blood dripping down their faces
shaking

As the world watches on
the army assembles
Against the oppressed
Powerless

The Tube

Nameless faces, strangers cluster together
Scruffy shirts half tucked in; eyes bleary
Stiletto heels poised in the perfume drenched air
The band of backpacks, cameras around necks
fatigued determination
Each waiting
Their minds adrift in their own secret worlds
Riddled with doubts, details, and dreams
Poker faces masking the stormscape beneath
Awaiting destiny's path

Instagram

What is happiness?
White weddings with wholesome warmth
Fulfilling festivities in far-flung fields
Vivid views on verdant vacations
Energetic exercising eagerly expressing enhancement
Polished posing for the perfect painted portrait
An unattainable universe
A spurious symbol
True happiness is far less sensuous
The hours spent talking in a car park
Or on a sofa at home in pyjamas
Meaningful connections

Career

How can I predict who I will be in thirty years' time?
Will I be grateful for my ambition?
Or weighed down by the climb?
Will I value a routine life?
Prioritising family, friends, and wildlife?
Managing life-or-death emergencies?
Or presenting lectures in universities?
There are so many things to think about
It's overwhelming, I'm close to bowing out

Pressure

The impending sense of doom
that threatens to clog up my throat
Unable to breathe
Forced to relive dark thoughts
Am I a failure?
Have I already failed at life?
Why do I feel I am constantly
running out of time
and breath
and life?
What makes a successful life?
Does it even matter?

Identity

The gap between the lines
The pause between words
Shining as bright as the sun
Dazzling darkness dances through the cracks
A constant state of flux
The taunt of outer peace

Faith

Do you see the beauty in the land?
Emerald green leaves gleaming in the light
Endless rolling waves stretching out to the sand
In perfect harmony and wisdom of His might
Magnificent mountains, pegs in the sky
Above fissuring thunder bellows out far
And wide as feathered wings glide, soar and fly
Into twinkling twilight as a shooting star
Shines hope and guidance from up above
The Almighty created beauty and peace
Send a light in the dark- of truth and love
Commanding unity, for pride to cease
Grateful for everything that surrounds me
Through faith-tinted lenses I live, breath and see

Sea

Remember this moment
Close your eyes
Feel my sand
embracing warmth between your toes
Feel my sun
its beaming glow lighting you up from within
Taste my salty air
my breezy breath whispering of adventures
Listen to my waves
soothing cocoons of calm
Freedom

Milton Keynes UK
Ingram Content Group UK Ltd.
UKHW032346150824
446941UK00011B/569